Bible Math: 2D and 3D Shapes

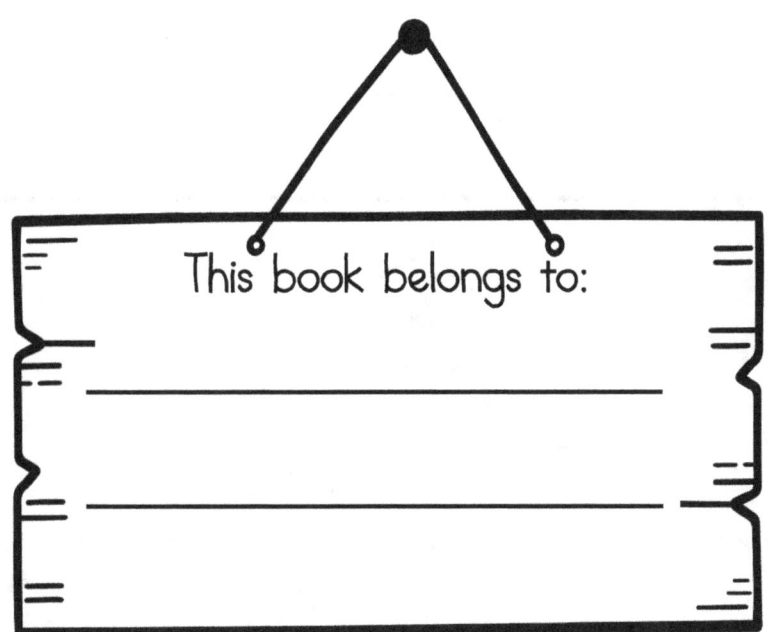

NOTE

Kindly note the interactive digital copies of Quail Publishers' products are on Boom Learning™. To access the interactive lessons:
- Sign up for Boom Learning at https://wow.boomlearning.com/ .
- Choose the free plan.
- Go to the store menu. Search for Quail Publishers.
- You can look for the 2D and 3D Shapes Boom Cards.
- Purchase the deck using Boom's points system.
- Go to library and you will see the deck.

Quail Publishers

The publisher grants teachers permission to photocopy pages from this book for classroom use only. Please purchase additional licenses if you are using it beyond your classroom. No other part of this publication may be reproduced, stored in a retrieval system or transmitted in any form or by any means, electronic, mechanical, photocopying, recording or otherwise, without the prior permission of the publisher.

Written and designed by Allison Hall
Bible Illustrations by Wayne Powell. Other illustrations sourced from Pixabay, Dreamstime and FreePik. Used under license.
Bible verses adapted from the Authorized King James Version
Text Copyright © 2023 by Allison Hall
All rights reserved. Published by Quail Publishers LLC, Coral Springs, Florida USA
Email: info@quailpublishers.com or quailpublishers@gmail.com
Website: www.quailpublishers.com

ISBN: 978-1-7376008-8-6

TABLE OF CONTENTS

Introduction 4

Circle 6

Square 8

Triangle 10

Rectangle 12

Diamond 14

Oval 16

Crescent 18

Star 20

2D Shapes Assessment 22

Sphere 32

Cube 34

Pyramid 36

Cuboid 38

Triangular Prism 40

Cylinder 42

Cone 44

3D Shapes Assessment 46

Shape Cards 53

Grid 55

INTRODUCTION

The early years of children's lives are very critical to their cognitive and physical development. It is therefore important that parents and teachers provide them with the necessary resources that foster this stage of their growth. The Bible Math: 2D and 3D Shapes workbook has engaging activities to promote Bible knowledge, and build children's early mathematic skills.

Using the Bible Math: 2D and 3D Shapes Activity Sheets

There are reproducible pages with learning activities that help children to understand all aspects of the two or three-dimensional shape being taught, as well as promote other early childhood concepts and skills. When children use the activity sheets they will:

- Identify and draw common 2D and 3D shapes
- Identify patterns and sequence
- Visual discriminate shapes
- Follow directions
- Perform hand-eye coordination
- Increase their mathematics vocabulary
- Improve their Bible Knowledge

The workbooks can be used in children's Bible classes and Christian schools' K-1 classrooms, as they are an excellent supplement for any early math program.

How to use the Activity Sheets

Before the Lesson
1. Review all aspects of the shape you will be teaching
2. Read the Bible story relating to the shape you will be teaching
3. Develop an exciting and engaging lesson which allows for multi-sensory activities
4. Integrate technology, using the interactive 2D and 3D Shapes Boom cards (see page 2)
5. Make sure that children have the necessary stationery and resources to participate in the lesson.
6. Ensure lessons have activities to foster home-school connections.
7. Be aware that some children will have more advanced early math knowledge than others. Use differentiated instruction to meet each child's needs.

Teaching the Lesson

1. **Shape Recognition**—Show children an example of the shape being taught. Shape cards are at the back of this book. Ask them to name the shape on the card.
2. **Shape Properties**—Discuss the properties or attributes of the specific shape. For example the number of corners and edges. Remind children that 2D shapes are flat, but 3D shapes are fat.
3. **Bible Knowledge**—Read the Bible story related to the shape. Discuss the story elements with students: theme, place, people, problem etc.
4. **Shape Knowledge**—Have children do the activities on the worksheets relating to the shape you are teaching.
5. **Home-School Connection**—Ask children to name objects in their environment that have similar shapes as the shape being taught.
6. **Reinforcement Strategies**—Use songs, rhymes and stories to reinforce the lesson taught. Build shapes from items such as sticks and clay.
6. **Assessment** - Use activities at the back of the book to assess children's understanding of geometric shapes, as well as other mathematical concepts and skills.
7. **Encouragement**—Encourage students always.

Properties of Geometric Shapes

Shape	Sides	Corners	Shape	Sides	Corners
circle	0	0	diamond	4	4
square	4	4	oval	0	0
triangle	3	3	crescent	0	0
rectangle	4	4	star	10	10

Shape	Faces	Edges	Vertices	Shape	Faces	Edges	Vertices
sphere	1	0	0	cube	6	12	8
pyramid	5	8	5	cuboid	6	12	8
cylinder	3	2	0	cone	2	1	1
Triangular prism	5	9	6				

Vertex = 1 corner or point
Vertices = more than one corner or point

Vertex/Vertices are corners or points where the line segments meet.
Edges are line segments that join vertices.
Face is the flat surface of the 3D shape.

Name: _____ Date: _____

○

circle

Trace and write.

circle

Story Time: Listen carefully as your teacher or parent reads the Bible story below. Color the object that has the same shape as a **circle**.

Bible Story: The Sun Stands Still
Bible Lesson: Joshua 10:1-15
Bible Theme: God Fights for Us

The Gibeonites were neighbors of the Jews. Five bad kings decided to join their armies to attack them. The Gibeonites sent a message to Joshua to come and help them. Joshua was the leader of the Jewish army. Joshua and his army quickly came to help the Gibeonites.

The Lord said to Joshua, "Do not be afraid for I have given them into your hand. Not one of them will be able to conquer you." Joshua's army fought the armies of the five bad kings. The Lord also made hailstone kill many of the soldiers in the bad kings' army. Joshua saw that the sun would go down soon. He did not want to fight in the dark. Joshua prayed to God for help. He then said, "Sun, stand still over Gibeon! O moon over the Valley of Aijalon!" That day, God made the sun stand still in the sky. The moon stopped too. The sun did not move until Joshua won the war. **God fights for us in times of trouble.**

Name: _____ Date: _____

Find the Shapes
Circle the objects that have the same shape as a circle.

Color them red.   Trace the lines.   Connect the dots.

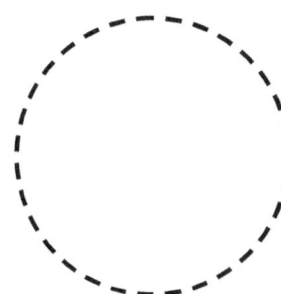 

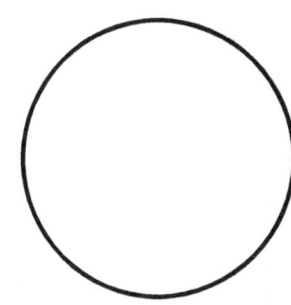 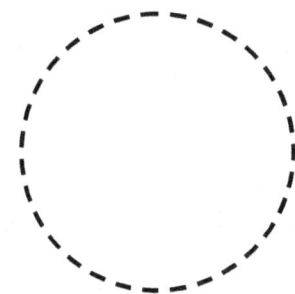 

2D Shape Properties. How many sides and corners does a **circle** have?

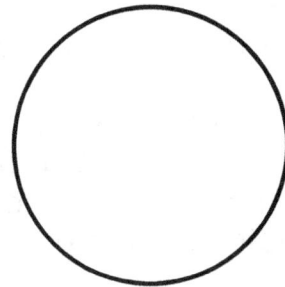

_____ sides

_____ corners

© Quail Publishers LLC 2023   Bible Math: 2D and 3D Shapes | 7

Name: _____ Date: _____

□ Trace and write.

square

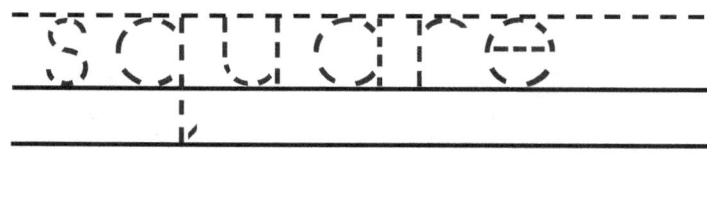

Story Time: Listen carefully as your teacher or parent reads the Bible story below. Color the object that has the same shape as a **square**.

Bible Story: The Breastplate
Bible Lesson: Joshua 10: 1-15
Ephesians 6:10-18
Bible Theme: Put On the Armor of God

The High Priest of Israel was the chief priest who stood for the people before God. Moses' brother Aaron was Israel's first High Priest. The High Priest wore a special uniform that was holy and beautiful. God told Moses how he wanted the clothes to be made.

One of the most beautiful objects on the uniform of the High Priest was the breastplate. The breastplate was also called the breastpiece of judgment. It had twelve precious stones set in gold. Each stone had the name of one of the twelve tribes of Israel.

Today, we have Jesus as our High Priest, and everyone can wear a breastplate. The Bible says that we should put on the breastplate of righteousness. This breastplate is a part of the Armor of God. God wants us to wear this armor every day. **God's armor protects us from Satan's evil attacks.**

Name: _____   Date: _____

Find the Shapes
Circle the objects that have the same shape as a **square**.

 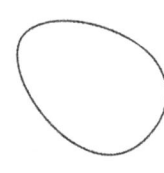 

Color them blue.   Trace the lines.   Connect the dots.

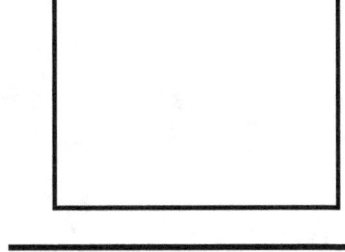 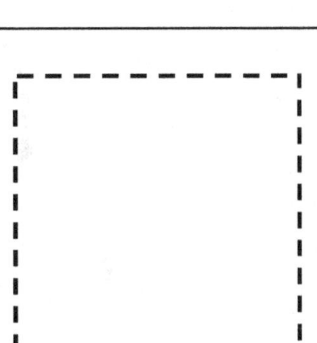

2D Shape Properties. How many sides and corners does a **square** have?

_____ sides

_____ corners

© Quail Publishers LLC 2023   Bible Math: 2D and 3D Shapes

Name: _____   Date: _____

Trace and write.

△
triangle

Story Time: Listen carefully as your teacher or parent reads the Bible story below. Color the object that has the same shape as a **triangle**.

Bible Story: The Temple of Artemis
Bible Lesson: Acts 19: 21-41
Bible Theme: Worship God, Not Statues

The Temple of Artemis was a big and beautiful building in Ephesus. Many people came there to worship the god Artemis. Apostle Paul preached to the citizens of Ephesus about Christ and many became Christians. This made the silversmiths in the city upset. These silversmiths made money from selling small statues of Artemis.

One day Demetrius, their leader, caused a riot in the city. He said, "My friends, you know we make good money from this business. But this man Paul is leading the people away from us. He says gods made from human hands are no good. We will soon lose our good name, and no one will respect the temple of our great goddess Artemis." The craftsmen shouted, "Great is Artemis of the Ephesians!" The crowd even seized two of Paul's friends and dragged them off to the theater. It took a city official a long time to calm the angry crowd. He told them that Paul had done nothing wrong. The city official told the crowd that if they continued to riot, they would be arrested. **We must always worship God and not idols.**

Name: _____ Date: _____

Find the Shapes
Circle the objects that have the same shape as a **triangle**.

 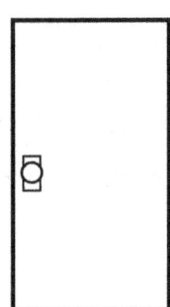 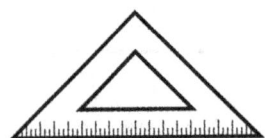

Color them yellow.   Trace the lines.   Connect the dots.

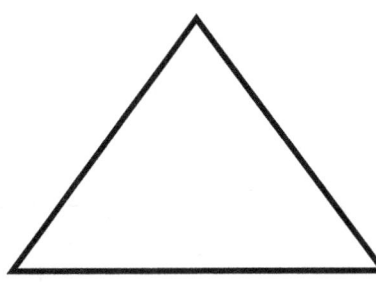 

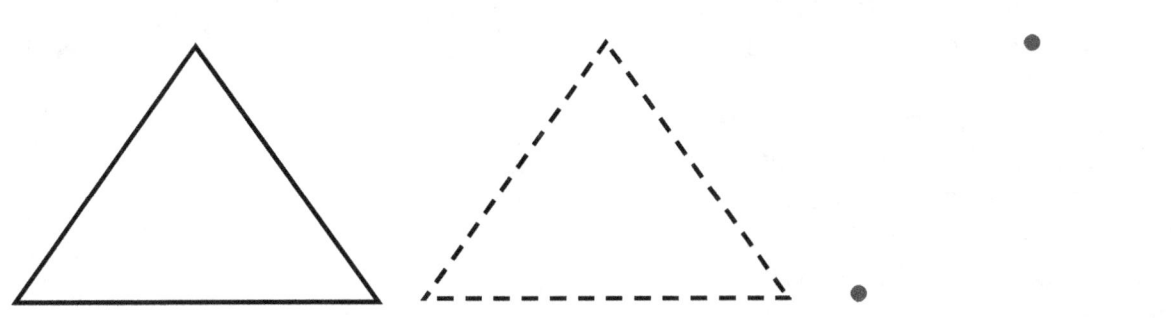

2D Shape Properties. How many sides and corners does a **triangle** have?

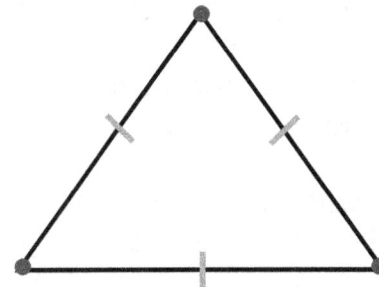

_____ sides

_____ corners

Name: _____   Date: _____

Trace and write.

rectangle

rectangle

Story Time: Listen carefully as your teacher or parent reads the Bible story below. Color the object that has the same shape as a **rectangle**.

Bible Story: The Passover Door
Bible Lesson: Exodus 11 and 12
Bible Theme: Obey God

The Israelites wanted to go to their new land in Canaan, that God promised them. But Pharoah of Egypt did not want them to go. He wanted them to stay as slaves of the Egyptians. God sent many plagues or diseases to punish the Egyptians. Still, Pharoah did not free the Israelites.

One day God told Moses that he would send one more plague on the Egyptians. God said, "Tonight I will go through Egypt and strike the firstborn of both people and animals. I will bring judgment on all the gods of Egypt, for I am the Lord." He told Moses to tell the Israelites to sacrifice a male lamb. They were to use a hyssop branch and dip it into the blood of the lamb. They would then use it to mark the doorpost of their homes. God said he will pass over the houses that were marked.

That night, a child died in every house with a doorpost that was not marked. Even Pharoah lost his firstborn child. There was loud crying all over Egypt. Pharoah told Moses and Aaron to take the Israelites and leave Egypt. He also asked Moses to bless him, but **God blesses us when we obey him.** The Israelites took all they had and then left for their new home.

Name: _____   Date: _____

Find the Shapes
Circle the objects that have the same shape as a rectangle.

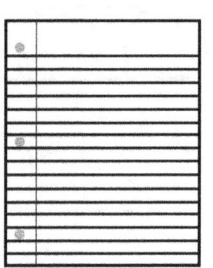 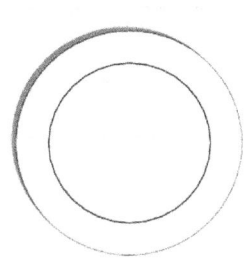 

Color them green.	Trace the lines.	Connect the dots.
	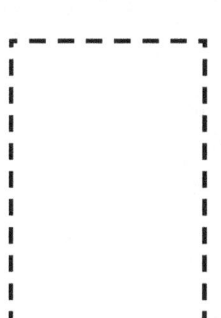	• • • •
		• • • •

2D Shape Properties. How many sides and corners does a **rectangle** have?

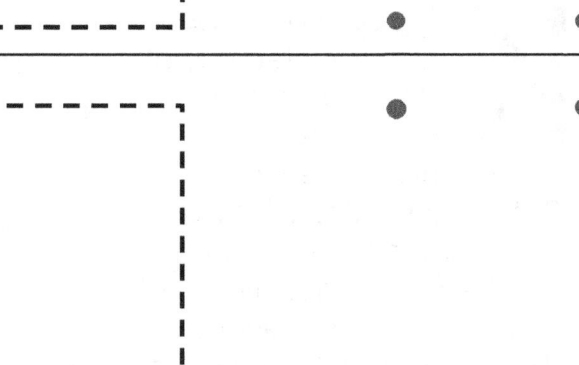

_____ sides

_____ corners

Name: _____ Date: _____

Trace and write.

diamond

diamond

Story Time: Listen carefully as your teacher or parent reads the Bible story below. Color the object that has the same shape as a **diamond**.

Bible Story: Saul Throws a Spear
Bible Lesson: 1 Samuel 19:1-17
Bible Theme: Do Not Be Jealous

King Saul of Israel was very jealous of David. He even told his son Jonathan and his officers to kill David. But Jonathan and David were friends. Jonathan told his father that he should not kill David for he had done nothing wrong. He told his father how David killed the giant Goliath and saved Israel. However, Saul was still jealous of David.

One day another war broke out between the Israelites and the Philistines. David went out and fought and won the war. Later, David went to King Saul's palace to play the harp for him. An evil feeling came upon King Saul, and he grew angry. He threw his spear at David and tried to pin him to the wall. David jumped out of the way quickly, and so the spear missed him. David then ran away to his home. Saul sent men to watch David's house. But David's wife, Princess Michal, helped him to escape before the men came to kill him. Michal was Saul's daughter. Saul was very angry with Michal for helping David to escape. **We must never be jealous of others, but treat everyone kindly.**

Name: _____ Date: _____

Find the Shapes
Circle the objects that have the same shape as a diamond.

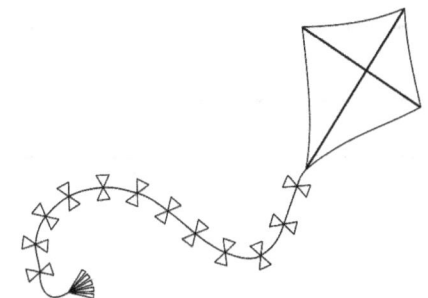  

Color them orange.   Trace the lines.   Connect the dots.

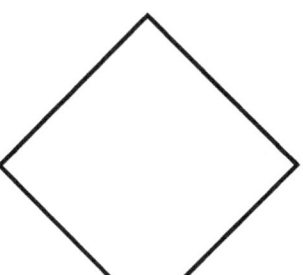 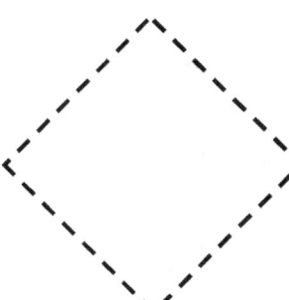

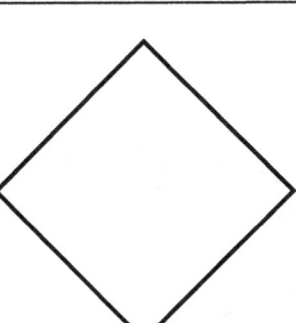 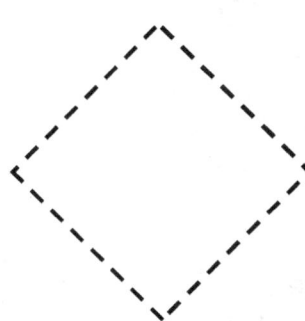 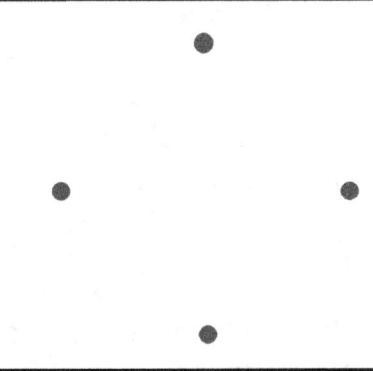

2D Shape Properties. How many sides and corners does a **diamond** have?

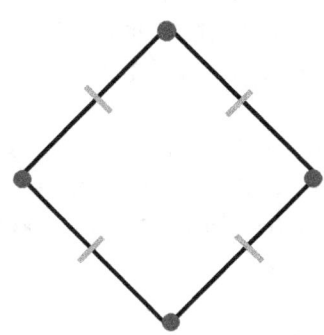

_____ sides

_____ corners

Name: _____   Date: _____

Trace and write.

oval

Story Time: Listen carefully as your teacher or parent reads the Bible story below. Color the object that has the same shape as an **oval**.

Bible Story: Eggs in the Nest
Bible Lesson: Deuteronomy 22:6-7
Bible Theme: Care for Others

Do you eat eggs? Many people do. Some people boil or fry their eggs. Others decorate them or use them in pastries. Eggs are also used in juices and as medicine.

Babies come from eggs. It is the first stage in the life cycle of most animals.

Some animals such as dogs, come from eggs that are inside their mothers' bodies. Other animals such as birds, come from eggs that are kept outside of their mothers' bodies.

Birds lay their eggs in nests. They then sit on them to keep them warm. They do this until they hatch into chicks.

The Bible says that we should not take the mother and all her eggs or chicks from a nest. We must therefore never take more than we need. In this way, we show that we care for others, even animals. **We must always care for all living things.**

Name: _____   Date: _____

Find the Shapes
Circle the objects that have the same shape as an **oval**.

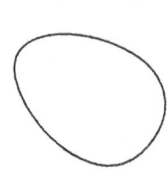  

Color them brown.	Trace the lines.	Connect the dots.
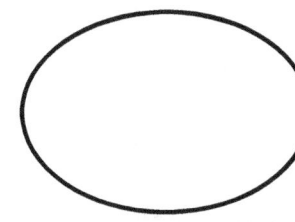		
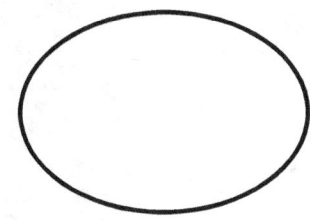	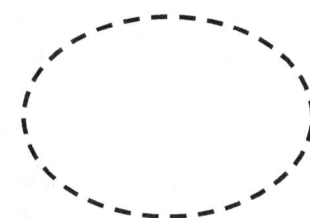	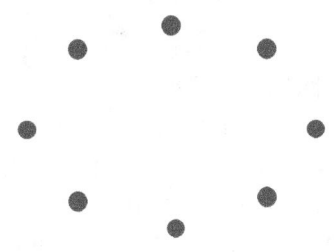

2D Shape Properties. How many sides and corners does an **oval** have?

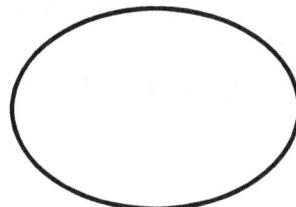   _____ sides

_____ corners

Name: _____ Date: _____

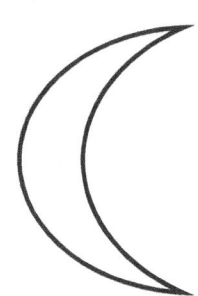

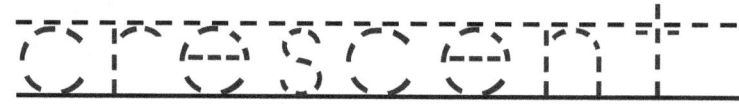

Trace and write.

crescent

Story Time: Listen carefully as your teacher or parent reads the Bible story below. Color the object that has the same shape as a **crescent**.

Bible Story: The Moon
Bible Lesson: Romans 12:1
Bible Theme: Believe in Jesus

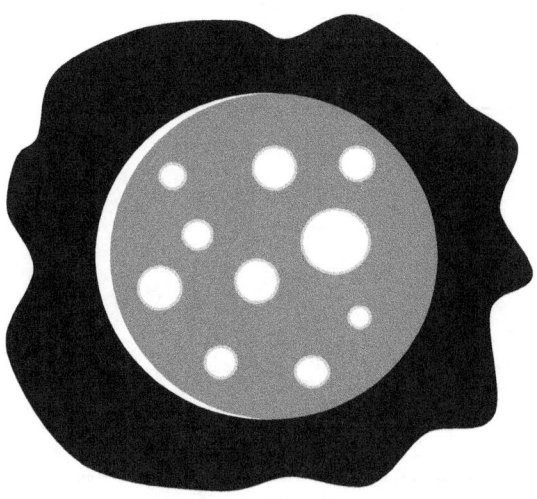

God made the moon on the fourth day of creation. The moon gives us light at night. It gets its light from the sun. The moon's light goes through different stages. The new moon is the first stage. You can hardly see the moon's crescent at this stage. The moon is full when it is round and very bright.

In ancient Israel, a new moon marked the beginning of a month. The Israelites held a new moon festival at this time. They would present offerings to God. Later, God did not want the offerings because the people were not obeying him.

Christians do not observe a new moon festival. They believe that Jesus became the new offering when he gave his life to save us.

Jesus is the Light of the World. **We get his light when we obey him and share his teachings.**

18 | © Quail Publishers LLC 2023 | Bible Math: 2D and 3D Shapes

Name: _____ Date: _____

Find the Shapes
Circle the objects that have the same shape as a crescent.

   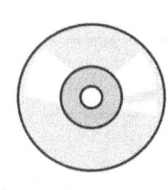   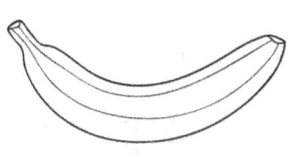

Color them gray.	Trace the lines.	Connect the dots.
		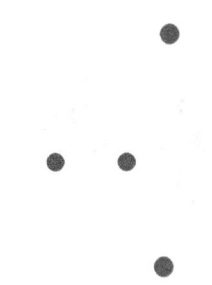

2D Shape Properties. A crescent is the part of a circle that is shown. How many sides and corners does a crescent have?

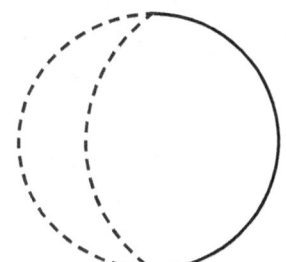

_____ sides

_____ corners

© Quail Publishers LLC 2023   Bible Math: 2D and 3D Shapes | 19

Name: _____ Date: _____

Trace and write.

star

Story Time: Listen carefully as your teacher or parent reads the Bible story below. Color the object that has the same shape as a **star**.

Bible Story: Star of Wonder
Bible Lesson: Matthew 2:1-12
Bible Theme: Obey God

Jesus was born in Bethlehem in Judea. On the night when he was born, a big, bright star lit up the night sky. It was so bright that even people from very far away saw it. Some of these people were a group of wise men who studied the stars. They came from very far just to meet Jesus.

When they arrived in Jerusalem, they sked, "Where is the child who is born King of the Jews? For we have seen his star in the east and have come to worship him." When King Herod heard this, he became very afraid. He asked the wise men to find Jesus. Herod told them to tell him when they had found Jesus, so that he could go and worship him. But Herod really wanted to kill Baby Jesus.

The bright star led the wise men to the house where Jesus and his family were. When they met Jesus, they worshipped him and gave him gifts of gold, frankincense, and myrrh. God later told the wise men in a dream, not to go back to King Herod, so they left for their country by another road. This made Herod very upset. **But God protects us when we obey him.**

20 | © Quail Publishers LLC 2023   Bible Math: 2D and 3D Shapes

Name: _____   Date: _____

Find the Shapes
Circle the objects that have the same shape as a **star**.

 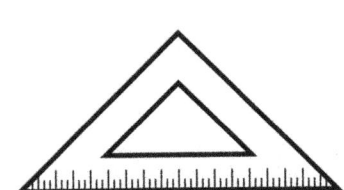 

Color them pink.   Trace the lines.   Connect the dots.

  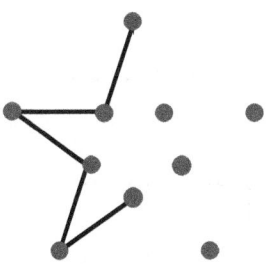

 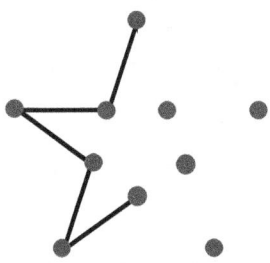

2D Shape Properties. How many sides and corners does a star have?

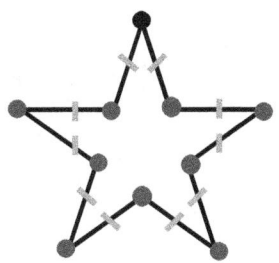

_____ sides

_____ corners

Name: _____ Date: _____

2D Shape Names: Draw a line to connect the each shape with its name.

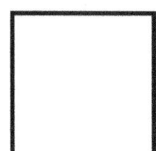   rectangle

   diamond

   circle

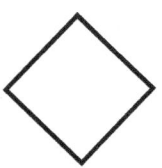   crescent

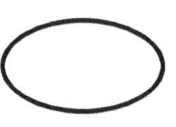   oval

   star

   triangle

square

Name: _____ Date: _____

2D Shapes In Our World: Draw a line to connect each object to its shape.

   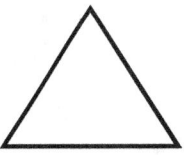

   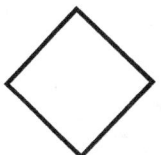

   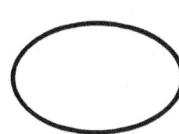

© Quail Publishers LLC 2023   Bible Math: 2D and 3D Shapes

Identifying Shapes.

Color the circles

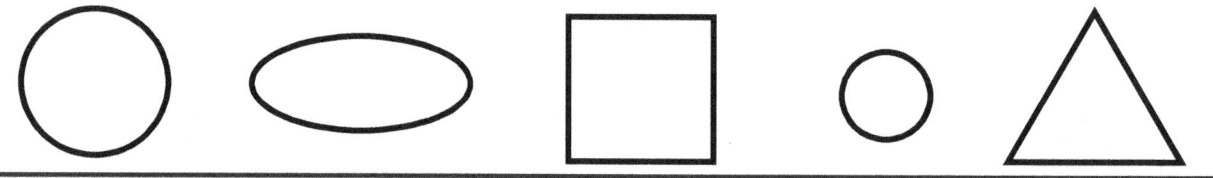

Color the squares

Color the triangles

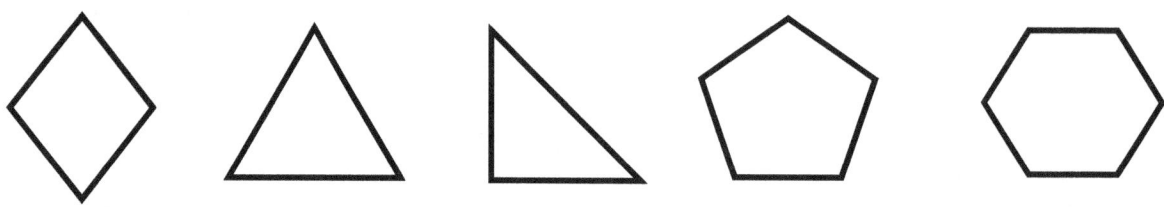

Color the rectangles

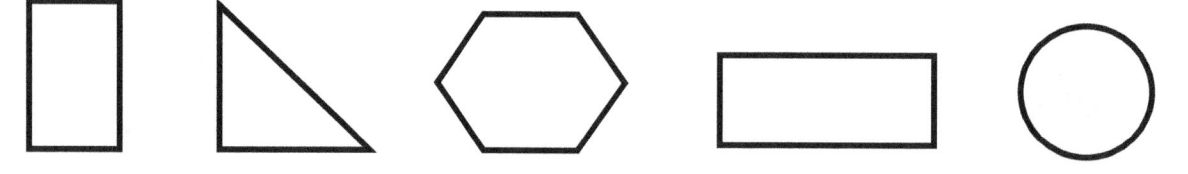

Color the ovals

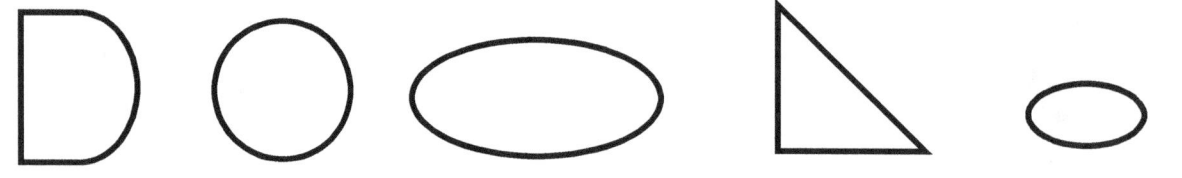

Color the crescents

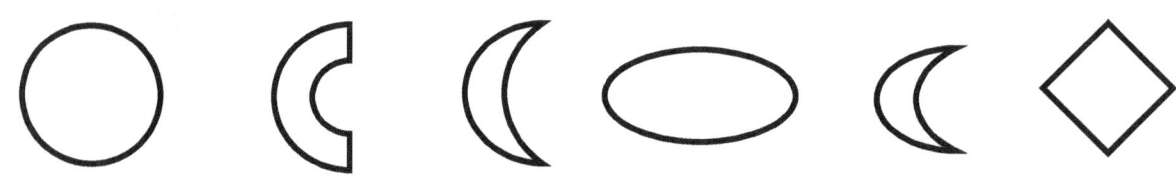

Name: _____ Date: _____

Shapes Properties: Compare the shapes.

Color the longest rectangle.

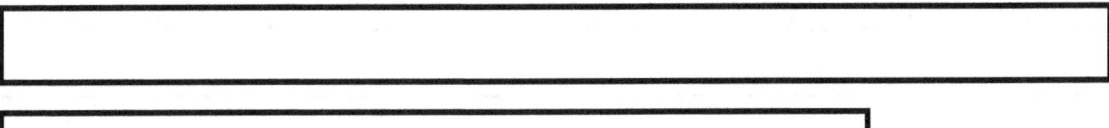

Color the tallest triangle.

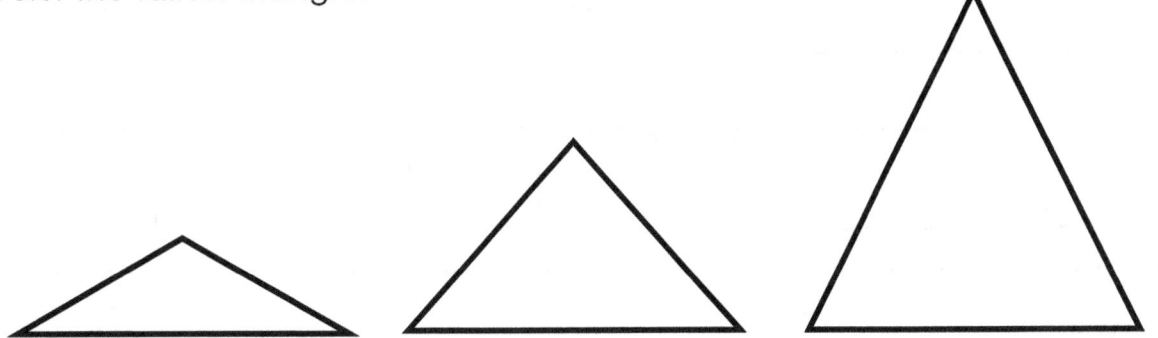

Color the shortest diamond.

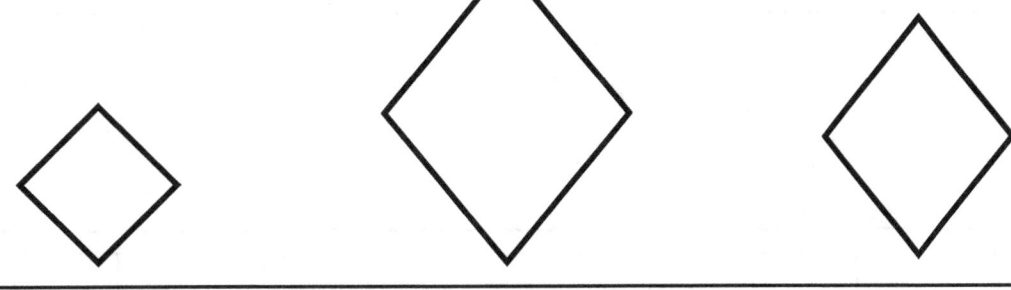

Color the biggest circle.

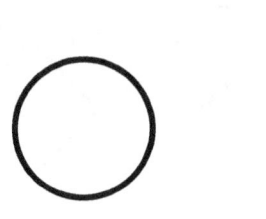 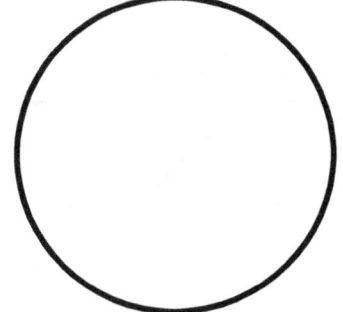 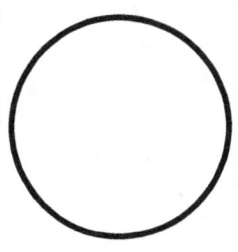

Name: _____   Date: _____

Odd 2D Shape Out! Look carefully at the shape patterns. Circle the shape that does not belong in each group.

  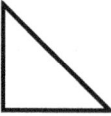  

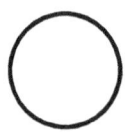  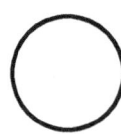 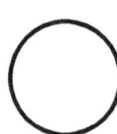 

   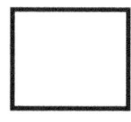 

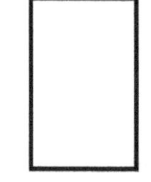 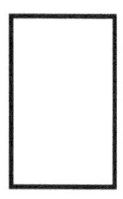 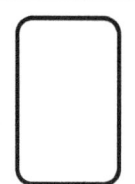 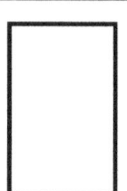 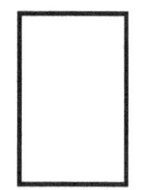

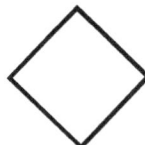 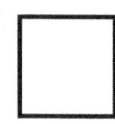 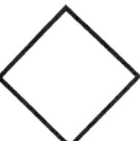  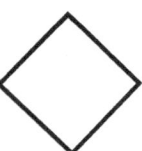

© Quail Publishers LLC 2023   Bible Math: 2D and 3D Shapes

Make them the Same. Find the incomplete picture, then complete the drawing to make it look like the others.

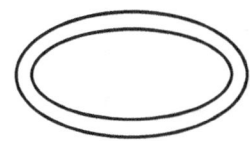 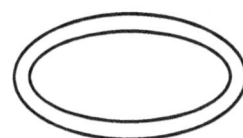 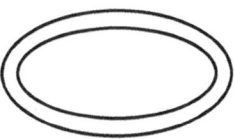 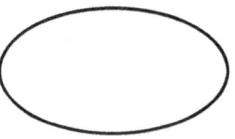

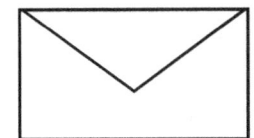 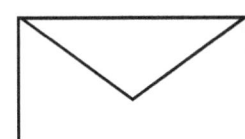 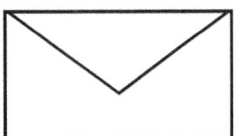 

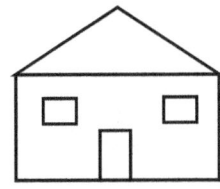   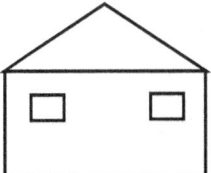

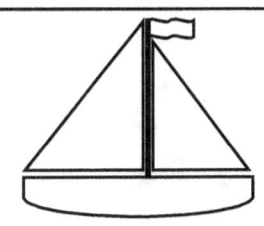 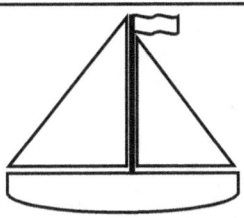 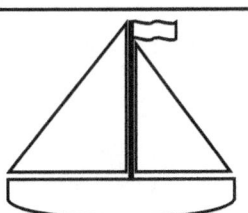 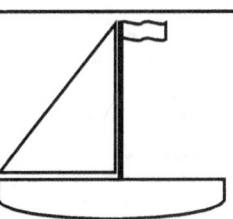

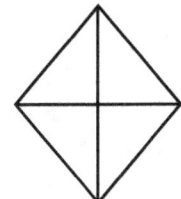 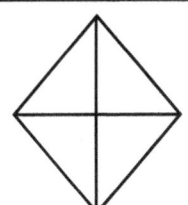 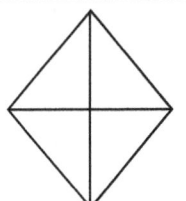 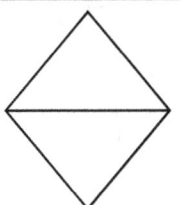

Name: _____ Date: _____

Shape Puzzle: Match the pieces to complete the shapes.

Piece A	Piece B	Shape
   	 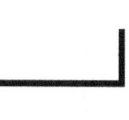    	 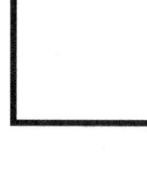 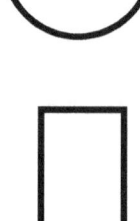 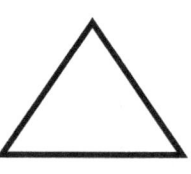 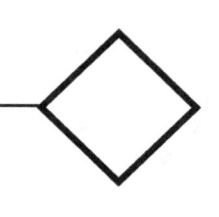  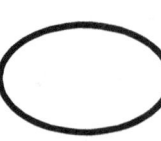

Name: _____ Date: _____

Spelling 2D Shape Names: Circle the correct spelling of each shape name.

○	cercle	circle
□	squire	square
△	triangle	triangel
▭	rektangle	rectangle
◇	dyamond	diamond
⬭	oval	oral
☾	crecent	crescent
☆	star	stare

Name: _____   Date: _____

Shape Patterns: Look carefully at the shape patterns. Then circle the shape that comes next in each group.

Name: _____ Date: _____

Complete the Shapes: Join the dots to complete the shapes, then color them.

Name: _____ Date: _____

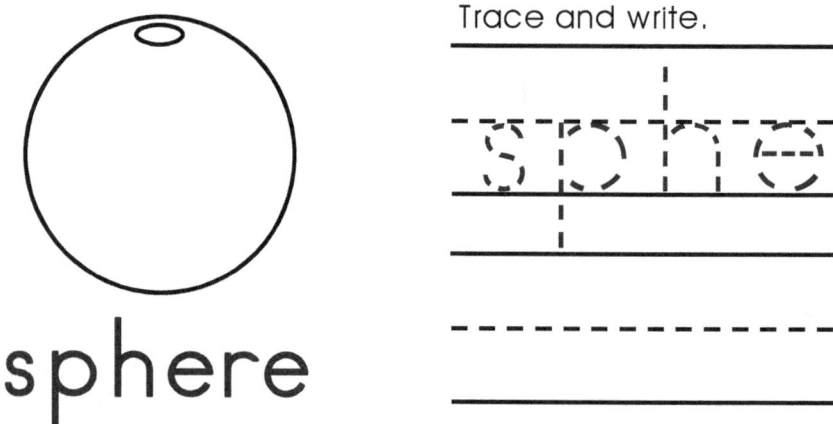

sphere

Story Time: Listen carefully as your teacher or parent reads the Bible story below. Color the object that has the same shape as a **sphere**.

Bible Story: The Earth is the Lord's
Bible Lesson: Genesis 1
Bible Theme: We are God's Stewards

Earth is one of the planets in our solar system. The Bible says that God created the earth and everything in it. In the beginning, the earth did not have any form and it was very dark. But God said, "Let there be light," and there was light. He separated the light from the dark. He called the light day and the darkness night. God put the sun and the moon above the earth to give us light.

God also made everything on the earth. God told Adam to take care of the everything on the earth. However, Adam and his wife Eve, were tricked by Satan. Sin entered the world because of them. Soon people started to treat the earth badly. They cut down trees and do not replant them. Some throw garbage in the wrong places and poison the earth. This harms animals and people.

We are stewards of the earth. A steward takes care of things. **God wants us to take care of the earth and all living things**. This brings glory to him and shows everyone that we love him.

Name: _____ Date: _____

Find the Shapes
Circle the objects that have the same shape as a **sphere**.

 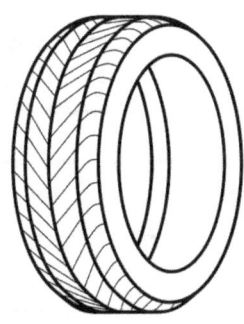 

Color them red.	Trace the lines.	Connect the dots.
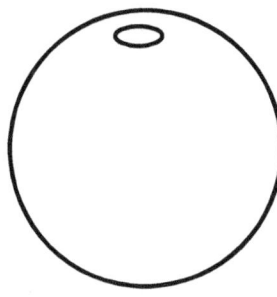	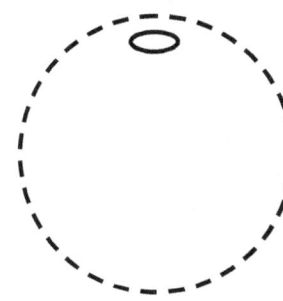	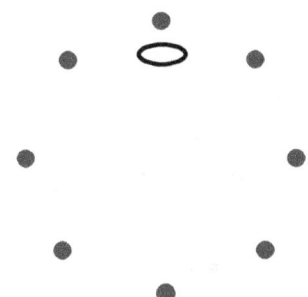
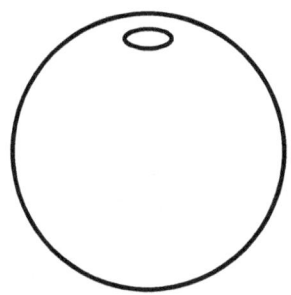	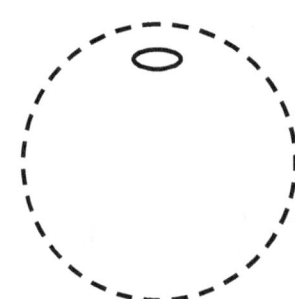	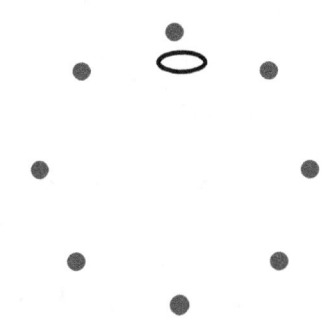

3D Shape Properties. Count each 3D shape property and write it below.

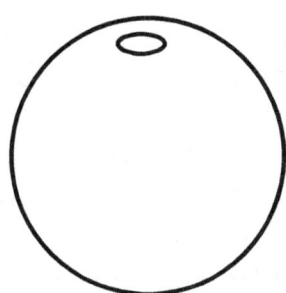

_____ face

_____ edges

_____ vertices

© Quail Publishers LLC 2023   Bible Math: 2D and 3D Shapes | 33

Name: _____ Date: _____

cube

Trace and write.

cube

Story Time: Listen carefully as your teacher or parent reads the Bible story below. Color the objects that have the same shape as a **cube**.

Bible Story: The Soldiers Cast Dice
Bible Lesson: Matthew 27:1-44
Bible Theme: Forgive Others

Jesus the Son of God came to earth to save us from our sins. He taught people how to be good and how they should worship God. However, the religious leaders did not like this. They told many lies about him and he was arrested. The Roman leaders knew that Jesus did nothing wrong, but they wanted to please the Jewish leaders and people. The people shouted, "Crucify him! Crucify him!" And so, Pilate told the soldiers to kill Jesus. The soldiers put a purple robe on him. They made a crown of thorns and put it on his head. The soldiers mocked him, beat him, and spat on him. They gave him a heavy cross to carry up a high hill. The soldiers then nailed him to the cross using big, sharp nails.

When they had killed him, the soldiers ripped his robe into pieces. They then gambled for the pieces by throwing dice. Although Jesus was treated unkindly, he was willing to die to save us. We must always be like Jesus. **We must forgive others, even those who are not kind to us.**

Name: _____ Date: _____

Find the Shapes
Circle the objects that have the same shape as a **cube**.

 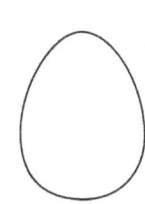 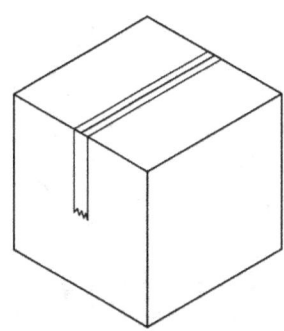

Color them blue.	Trace the lines.	Connect the dots.
	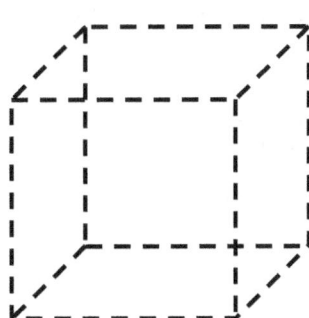	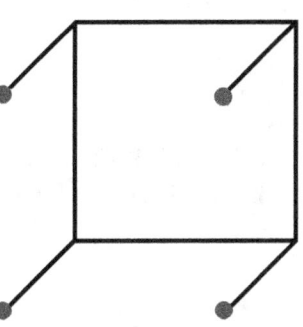
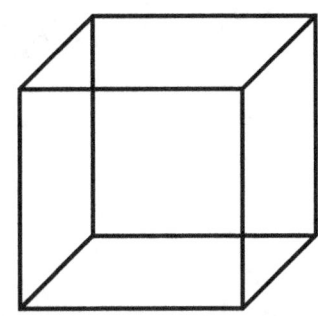	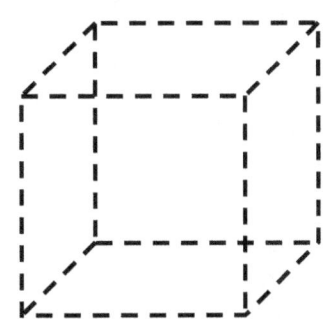	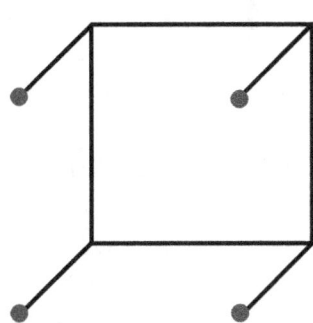

3D Shape Properties. Count each 3D shape property and write it below.

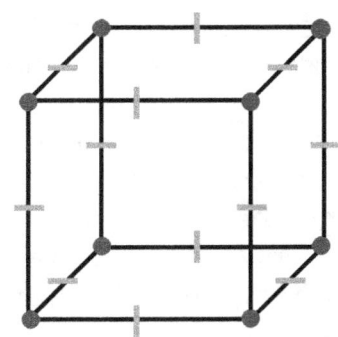

_____ faces

_____ edges

_____ vertices

Name: _____ Date: _____

pyramid

Trace and write.

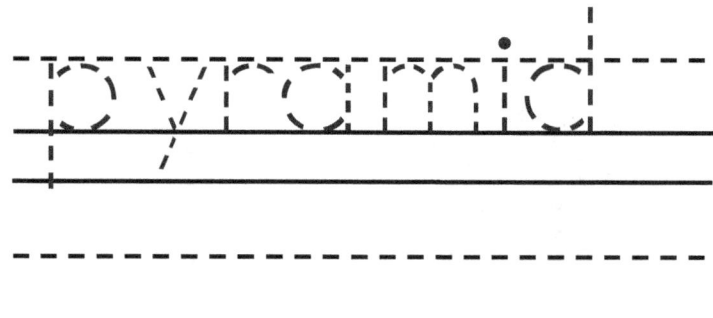

Story Time: Listen carefully as your teacher or parent reads the Bible story below. Color the objects that have the same shape as a **pyramid**.

Bible Story: Moses Flees Egypt
Bible Lesson: Exodus 2:11-15
Bible Theme: Never Hurt Others

Moses was a prince in Egypt. He was the son of Pharaoh's daughter, who adopted him when he was young. Although he was a prince, he always knew that his parents were Hebrews. The Pharaoh of Egypt had made the Hebrews slaves because they had grown into a strong and healthy tribe.

One day Moses went to the place where the Hebrews were working. Moses saw an Egyptian beating a Hebrew. He was very angry. Moses looked around and thought that no one else was nearby. He then killed the Egyptian slave master and pushed his body under the sand. The next day when he tried to stop a fight between two Hebrews, one of the men said, "Who made you ruler and judge over us? Are you going to kill me like how you killed the Egyptian?" Moses was very afraid, as what he did was now known.

When Pharaoh heard about what Moses had done, he tried to kill him. Moses quickly ran away from Egypt to Midian, a desert town.

Moses lived in Midian for many years. While he was there, he became a shepherd, got married, and had a family. He only returned to Egypt when God told him to. **We must never hurt others, even when we are angry.**

Name: _____ Date: _____

Find the Shapes
Circle the objects that have the same shape as a **pyramid**.

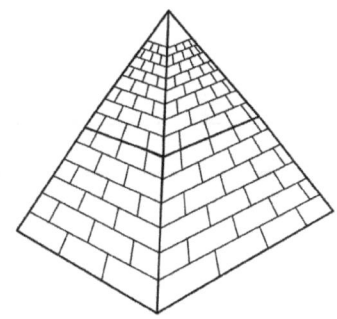  

Color them yellow. Trace the lines. Connect the dots.

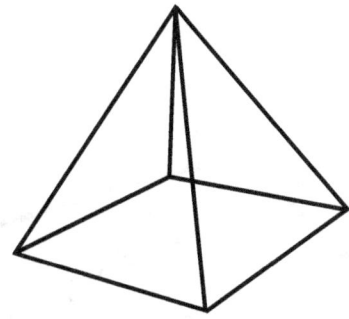 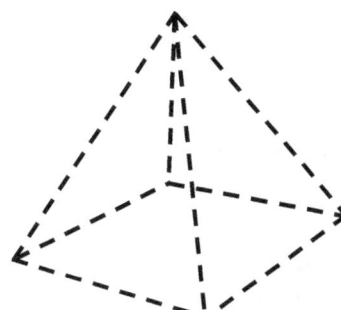 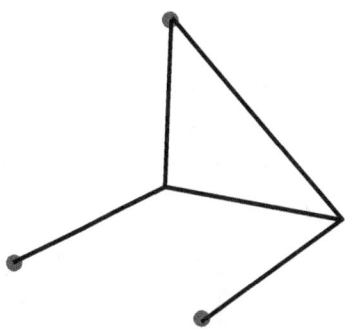

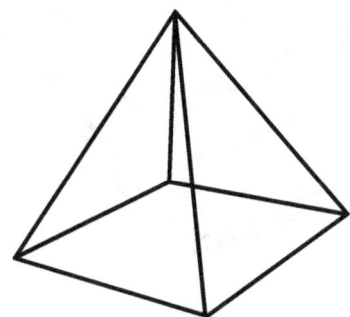 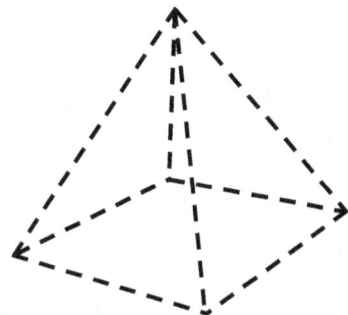 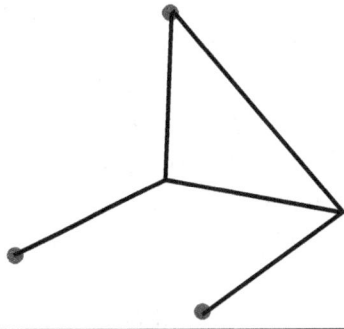

3D Shape Properties. Count each 3D shape property and write it below.

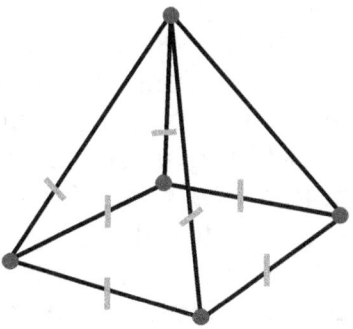

_____ faces

_____ edges

_____ vertices

Name: _____ Date: _____

Trace and write.

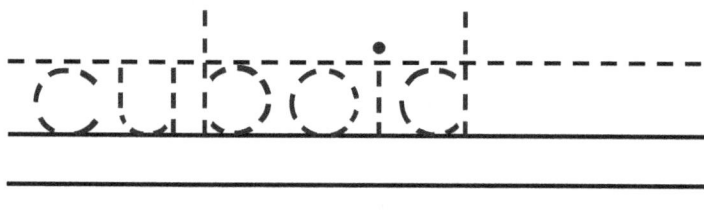

cuboid

Story Time: Listen carefully as your teacher or parent reads the Bible story below. Color the object that has the same shape as a **cuboid**.

Bible Story: The Book of Books
Bible Lesson: Jeremiah 36:2
Bible Theme: Study God's Word

The Bible is a book with many books. It is the holy book of the Christian religion. People all over the world read the Bible and follow its teachings. Even people who are not Christians, love the teachings of the Bible and follow them too. The Bible teaches us what is right, from what is wrong. It also shows us how to be followers of Jesus Christ.

The Bible has two parts called, the Old Testament and the New Testament. The Jews call the Old Testament, the Tanakh. The Bible has poems, stories, letters, prayers, songs, proverbs, and God's laws. It gives us information on the history of the world and on daily living.

God inspired men to write the Bible. These men wrote Bible verses on stones, clay tablets, and scrolls. Later, these verses were printed in books. The writers lived at different times and had many different jobs. Some were farmers, shepherds, kings, prophets, fishermen, and judges. It took more than a thousand years to write the Bible. Many people were killed for writing the Bible in other languages. Others were killed for reading the Bible.

Today, we can read the Bible in many languages. It is still the best-selling book in the world. **You should read the Bible and follow its teachings.**

Name: _____   Date: _____

Find the Shapes
Circle the objects that have the same shape as a **cuboid**.

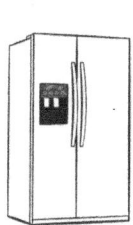 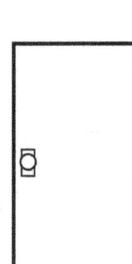 

Color them green.   Trace the lines.   Connect the dots.

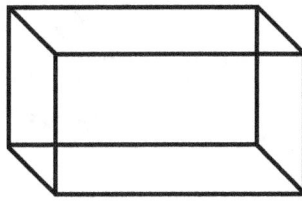 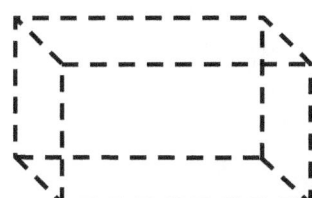 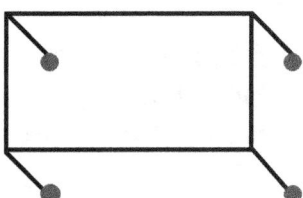

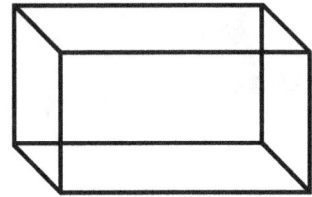 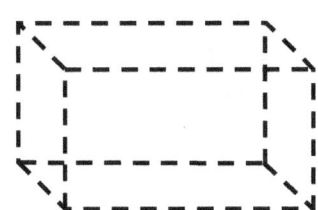 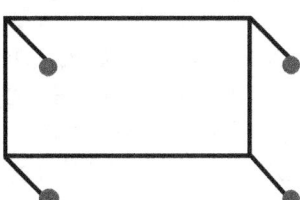

3D Shape Properties. Count each 3D shape property and write it below.

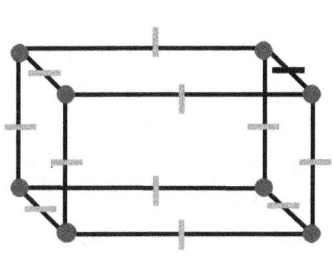

_____ faces

_____ edges

_____ vertices

Name: _____ Date: _____

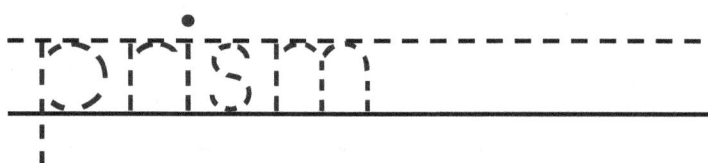

Trace and write.

triangular prism

Story Time: Listen carefully as your teacher or parent reads the Bible story. Color the object that has the same shape as a **triangular prism**.

Bible Story: Angels Visit Abraham
Bible Lesson: Genesis 18:1-16
Bible Theme: Be Faithful

One hot day Abraham was sitting in front of his tent when he saw three men standing nearby. He quickly got up and greeted the men. Abraham offered them water to wash their feet and food to eat. The men accepted Abraham's kindness. Abraham hurried into his tent to get the things prepared. He told his wife Sarah to prepare bread and asked his servant to choose a tender calf to prepare as meat. While they were eating, one of the men said to Abraham, "I will return about this time next year. Also, your wife Sarah will have a son."

Sarah who was listening, laughed to herself. She said, "I'm so worn out, and my husband is old. Can I really know the joy of having a baby?"

The man then said to Abraham, "Why did Sarah laugh? Why did she say, 'Will I really have a baby, now that I am so old?' Is anything too hard for the Lord? Anyway, I will return at the appointed time next year. And Sarah will indeed have a son." Sarah was now afraid and so she lied and said, "I didn't laugh." But the man said, "Yes, you laughed." The men then left for another city. **We must never tell lies but have faith in God.**

Name: _____ Date: _____

Find the Shapes
Circle the objects that have the same shape as a **triangular prism**.

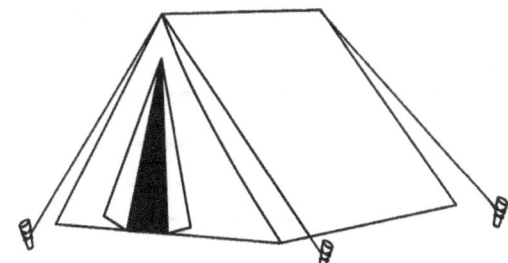 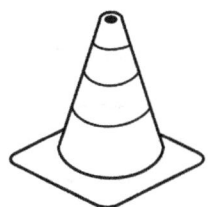 

Color them orange.   Trace the lines.   Connect the dots.

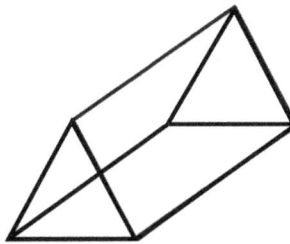 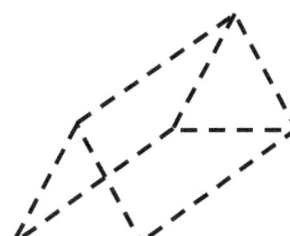 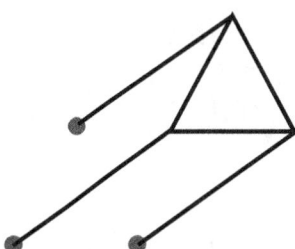

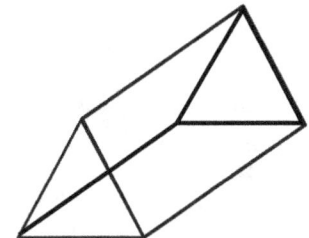 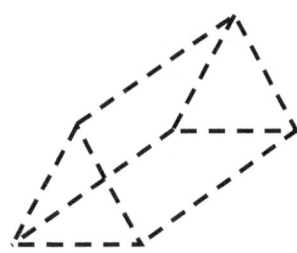 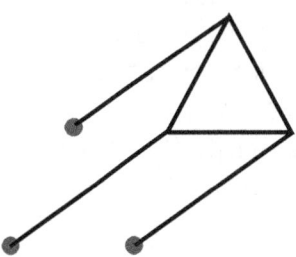

3D Shape Properties. Count each 3D shape property and write it below.

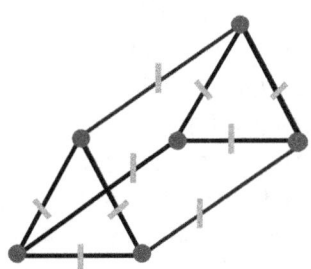

_____ faces

_____ edges

_____ vertices

Name: _____ Date: _____

Trace and write.

cylinder

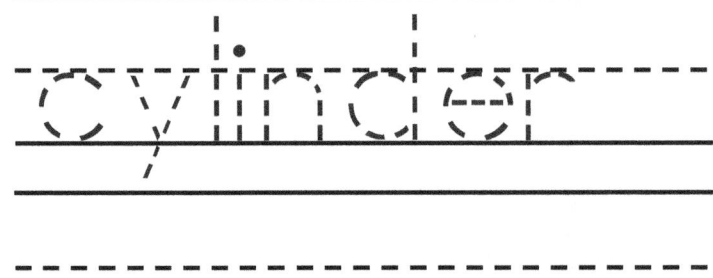

Story Time: Listen carefully as your teacher or parent reads the Bible story below. Color the objects that have the same shape as a **cylinder**.

Bible Story: Strong Samson
Bible Lesson: Judges 16:4-30
Bible Theme: Rely on God's Power

Long ago, in Israel, there lived a man named Manoah. One day an angel appeared to his wife and told her that she would have a very special son. The angel told Manoah's wife to eat special foods and drink no alcohol while she was pregnant. The angel also told her not to cut her son's hair, as it would be a sign that he has the Spirit of God.

Manoah and his wife named their son Samson. He grew into a strong man with very long hair. He fought and killed many Philistines. This made the Philistines hate and fear him. Samson later fell in love with a Philistine woman named Delilah. She tricked him into telling her the secret of his strength. She then had a man cut off his hair while he slept. When the Philistines attacked, Samson could not fight back. They dug out his eyes and put him in prison.

One day the Philistines gathered at the temple of their god Dagon, to praise him for helping them to capture Samson. They took Samson into the temple and mocked him. Samson prayed to God for strength one more time, to punish the Philistines for blinding him. God gave back Samson his strength. He pushed down the pillars that held up the temple. The building fell and killed all the Philistines. **We must always rely on God's power.**

Name: _____ Date: _____

Find the Shapes
Circle the objects that have the same shape as a **cylinder**.

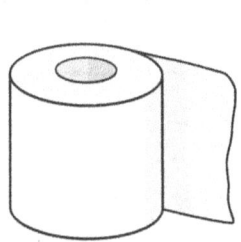 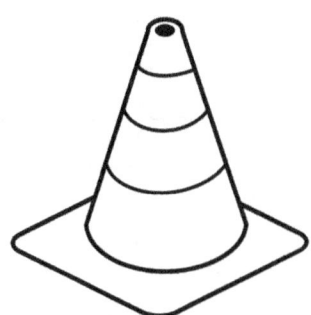 

Color them purple.   Trace the lines.   Connect the dots.

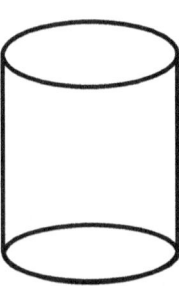 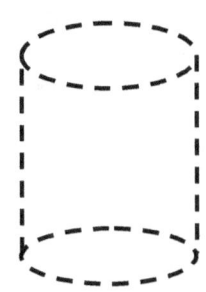 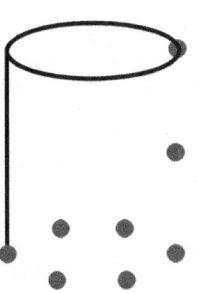

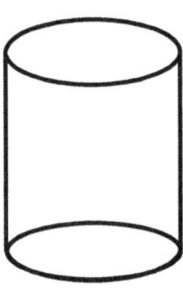 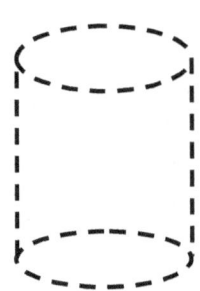 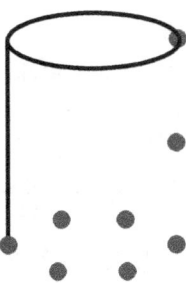

3D Shape Properties. Count each 3D shape property and write it below.

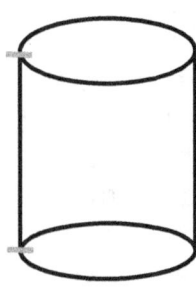

_____ faces

_____ edges

_____ vertices

Name: _____   Date: _____

Trace and write.

cone

Story Time: Listen carefully as your teacher or parent reads the Bible story below. Color the object that has the same shape as a **cone**.

Bible Story: God Comes in a Whirlwind
Bible Lesson: Book of Job
Bible Theme: Have Faith in God

In the land of Uz, there once lived a rich man named Job who loved God. One day Satan told God that the only reason why Job worshipped him was because he had life easy. Satan also said God was protecting Job. So, God said to Satan, do anything you want to Job, except kill him. The wicked angel caused Job's children, and most of his servants and animals to die. Job was very sad. He tore his robe, shaved his head, fell to the ground, and shouted, "The Lord has given, and he has taken away. Blessed is the name of the Lord." Despite what happened, Job remained faithful to God.

One day Job's friends came to visit him. They did not recognize him at first. Job had sores and scratches all over his body. Job's friends stayed for a week without even saying a word to him. They thought that Job had sinned and so God was punishing him. However, Job told them that they were wrong. God then appeared to Job and his friends out of a whirlwind. God was angry with Job's friends for not speaking the truth. Job prayed to God to forgive his friends. God forgave them and later gave back Job all that he had lost. **We must always remain faithful to God even in hard times.**

Name: _____ Date: _____

Find the Shapes
Circle the objects that have the same shape as a **cone**.

 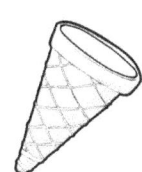 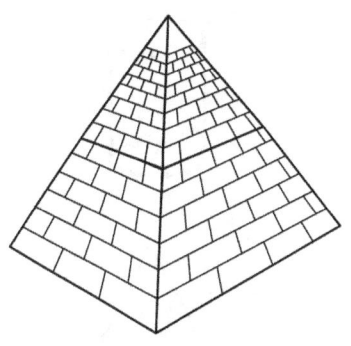

Color them pink.   Trace the lines.   Connect the dots.

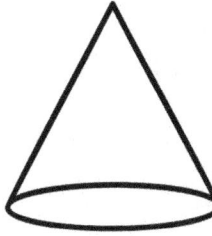 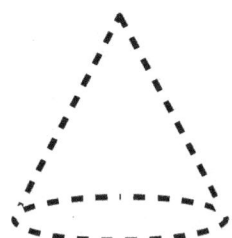 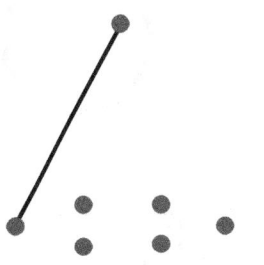

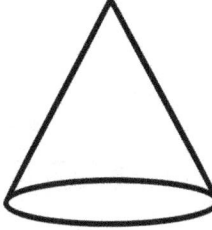 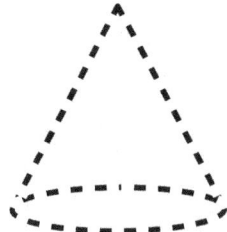 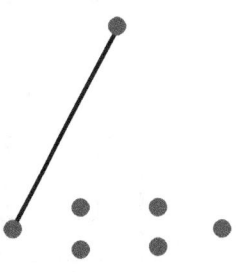

3D Shape Properties. Count each 3D shape property and write it below.

_____ faces

_____ edge

_____ vertex

© Quail Publishers LLC 2023   Bible Math: 2D and 3D Shapes | 45

3D Shape Names: Draw a line to connect the each 3D shape with its name.

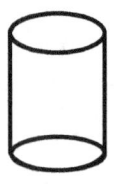

sphere

cuboid

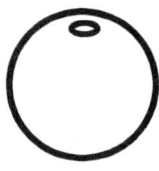

cube

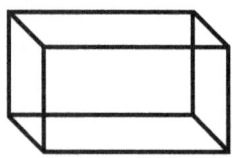

pyramid

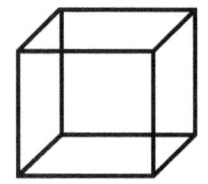

cylinder

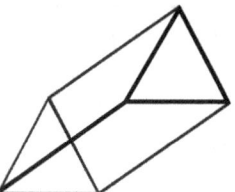

cone

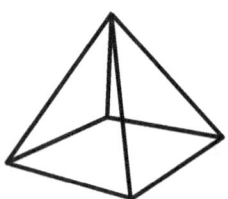

triangular prism

Name: _____ Date: _____

3D Shape Nets: Draw a line to connect the each 3D shape with its net. The net is what the 3D shape would look like if it were opened out and laid flat.

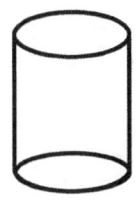

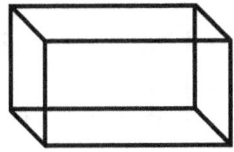
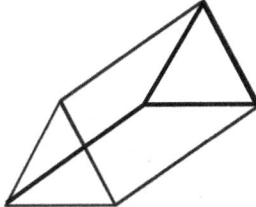
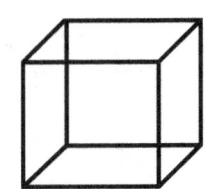
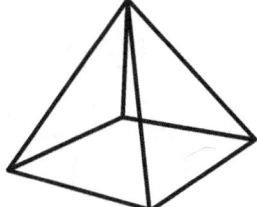

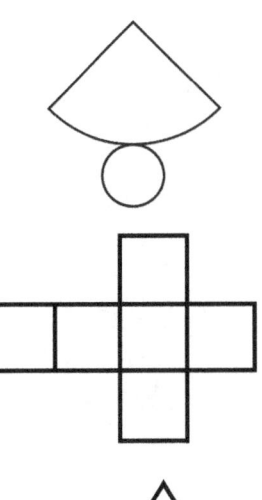

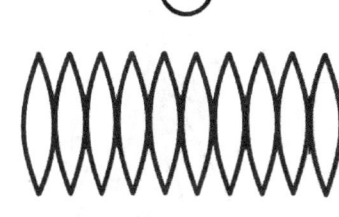
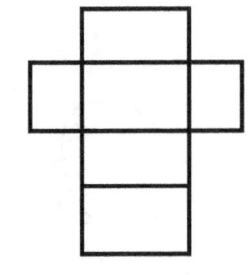
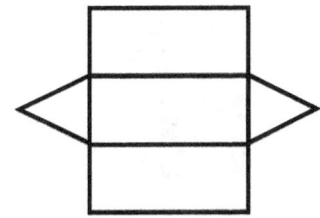

© Quail Publishers LLC 2023 — Bible Math: 2D and 3D Shapes

Name: _____ Date: _____

3D Shapes in Our World: Draw a line to connect each object to its shape.

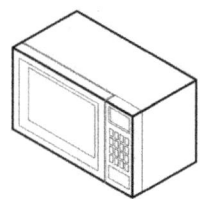

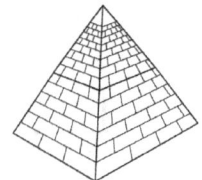
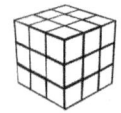
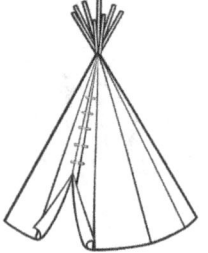

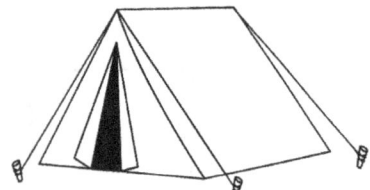

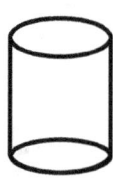

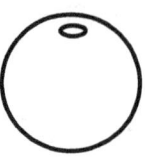
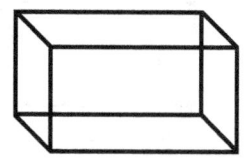
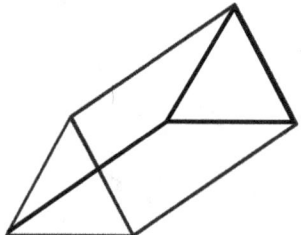
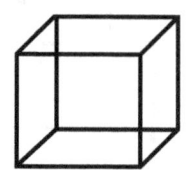
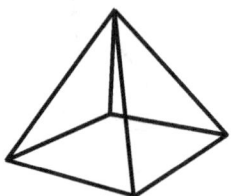

2D and 3D Shapes Match: Draw a line to match each 2D shape to its 3D shape look-a-like.

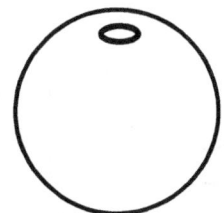

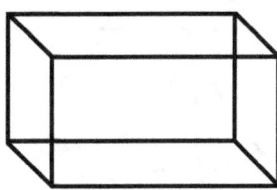

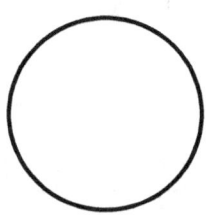
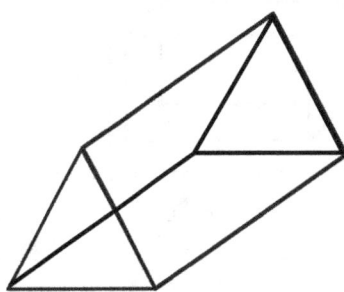

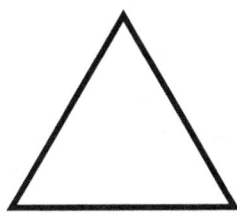
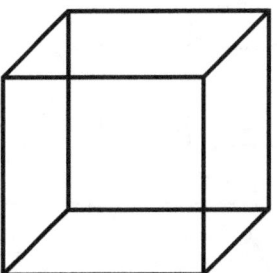

Name: _____ Date: _____

Spelling 3D Shape Names: Circle the correct spelling of each shape name.

(sphere)	sphere	sfere
(cube)	cub	cube
(pyramid)	pyramide	pyramid
(cuboid)	cuboid	cueboid
(triangular prism)	triangular prysm	triangular prism
(cylinder)	cilinder	cylinder
(cone)	cone	coan

Name: _____   Date: _____

Complete the Pictures. Look carefully at the pictures in each group. Then circle the picture that comes next to show the completed object.

3D Shapes: Stack, Roll and Slide

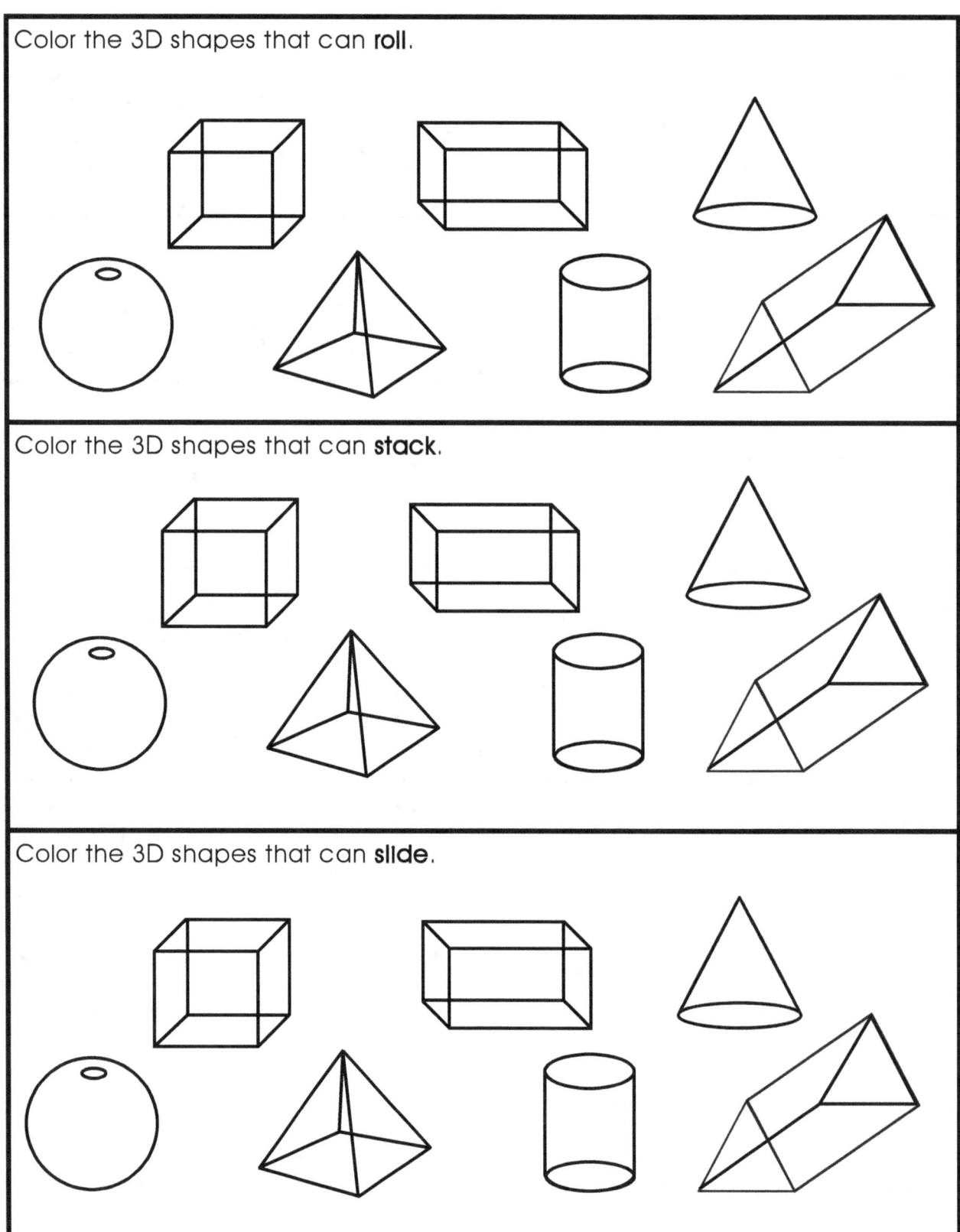

Name: _____   Date: _____

2D Shape Cards: Teachers! Parents! Copy and cut the cards, then use them to teach children about 2D shapes.

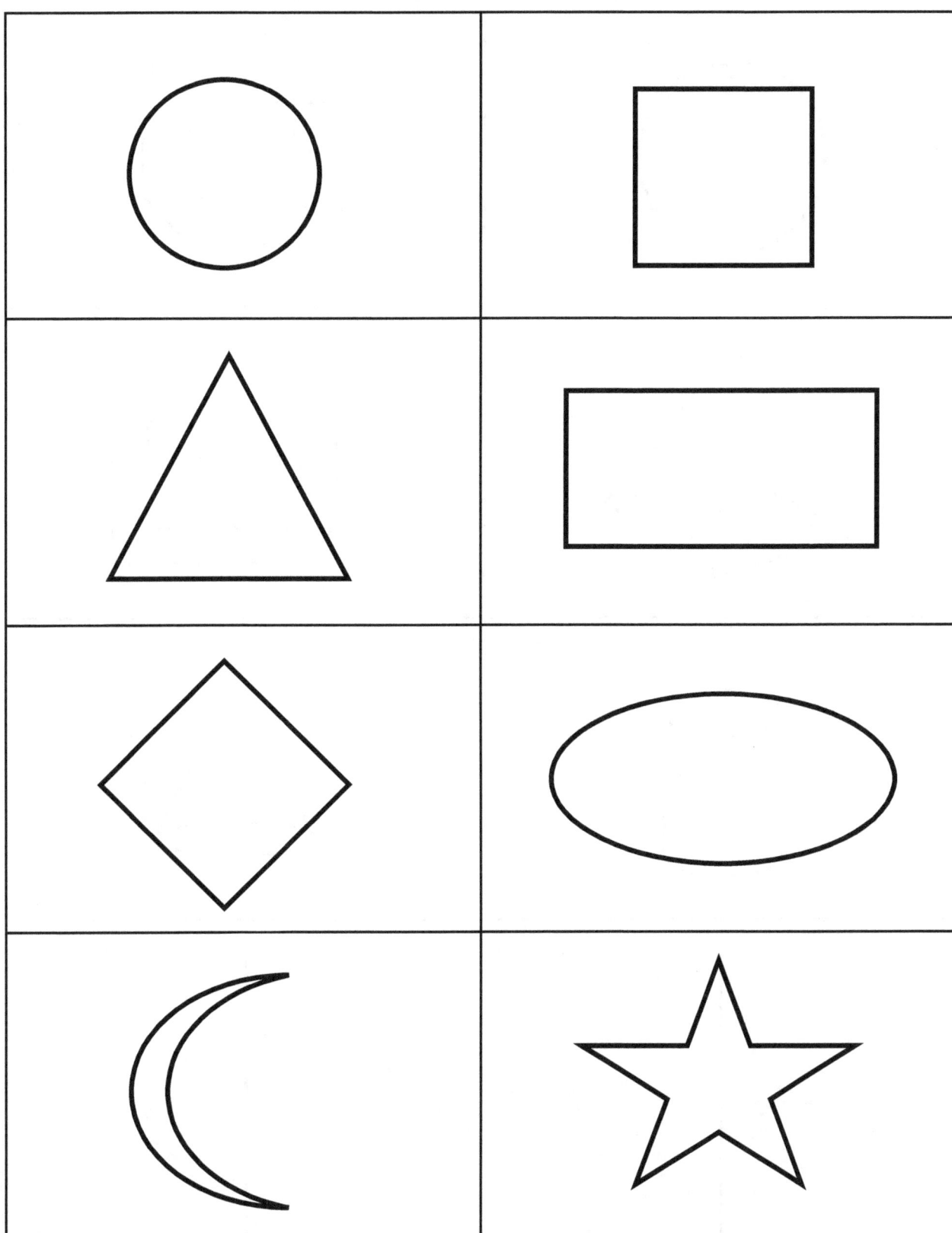

© Quail Publishers LLC 2023

Name: _____ Date: _____

3D Shape Cards: Teachers! Parents! Copy and cut the cards, then use them to teach children about 3D shapes.

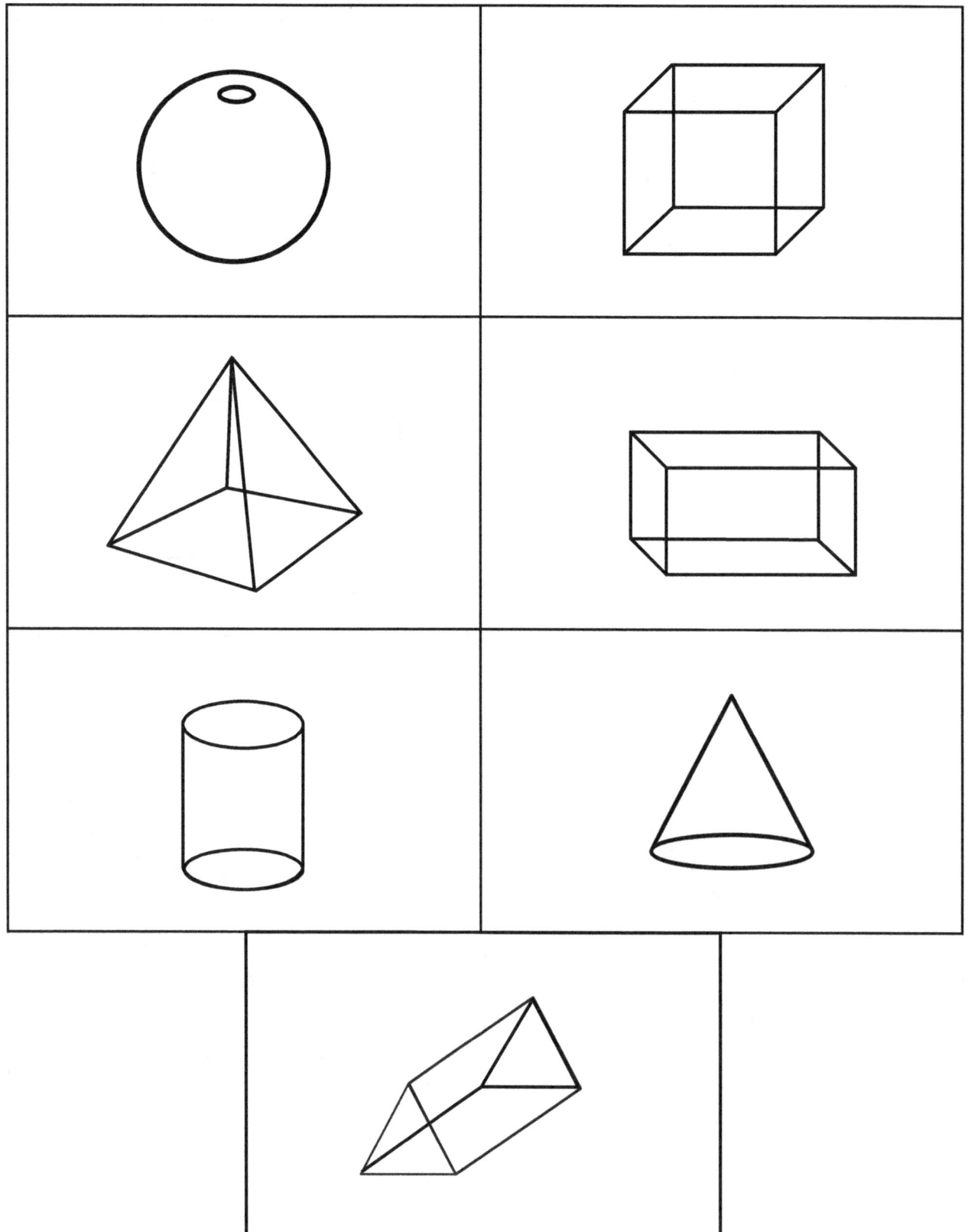

Name: _____   Date: _____

Dot Grid: Use the grid to draw 2D and 3D shapes.